Date: _______________________

Created especially for you

Date: ______________________________

Created especially for you

Everyone needs
'A Little Black Book'.
A place to write 'secret
things' and to write 'stuff'
that you think about and
want to remember - and
not want to remember.
'A Little Black Book' is that
prized and treasured
notebook
that you keep close to your
heart.
The 'Little Black Book' that
takes you on journeys of
memories - and prepares
you for the next one.
Everything you need will be
in here.

Created especially for
you.....

Date: _______________________

Created especially for you

Date: _______________________

Created especially for you

Date: ___________________________

Created especially for you

Date: ________________________

Date: ___________________________________

Created especially for you

Date: _______________________________

Created especially for you

Date: ______________________

Created especially for you

Date: _______________________________

Created especially for you

Date: _______________________

Date: _______________________________

Date: ______________________________

Created especially for you

Date: _______________________

Created especially for you

Date: _______________________________

Date: ___________________________

Date: _______________________________

Date: ____________________________

Date: _______________________

Date: _______________________________

Created especially for you

Date: ______________________________

Created especially for you

Date: _______________________

Created especially for you

Date: ______________________________

Created especially for you

Date: ______________________________

Created especially for you

Date: _______________________

Date: _______________________

Created especially for you

Date: ________________________________

Created especially for you

Date: _______________________________

Created especially for you

Date: ___________________________

Date: _______________________

Created especially for you

Date: _______________________

Created especially for you

Date: _______________________________

Created especially for you

Date: _______________________

Created especially for you

Date: ______________________________

Date: _______________________________

Date: _______________________________

Created especially for you

Date: _______________________________

Created especially for you

Date: _______________________________

Created especially for you

Date: _______________________

Created especially for you

Date: ______________________________

Created especially for you

Date: _______________________________

Date: _______________________

Created especially for you

Date: _______________________

Date: _______________________________

Date: _______________________________

Created especially for you

Date: _______________________________

Created especially for you

Date: ______________________

Created especially for you

Date: ___________________________

Created especially for you

Date: ________________________

Created especially for you

Date: ___________________________

Created especially for you

Date: _______________________

Date: ____________________________

Created especially for you

Date: ______________________________

Created especially for you

Date: _______________________________

Created especially for you

Date: _______________________

Date: _______________________________

Date: _______________________________

Date: _______________________________

Created especially for you

Date: ______________________________

Date: _______________________

Created especially for you

Date: _______________________________

Created especially for you

Date: _______________________

Created especially for you

Date: ________________________________

Created especially for you

Date: ___________________________

Created especially for you

Date: ____________________________

Date: _______________________________

Created especially for you

Date: ___________________________________

Created especially for you

Date: _______________________________

Created especially for you

Date: ___________________________

Date: ________________________

Created especially for you

Date: ________________________________

Created especially for you

Date: _______________________________

Created especially for you

Date: _______________________

Created especially for you

Date: ______________________________

Created especially for you

Date: _______________________________

Created especially for you

Date: _______________________________

Date: _______________________________

Created especially for you

Date: _______________________

Created especially for you

Date: _______________________

Date: _______________________

Created especially for you

Date: _______________________________

Date: _______________________________

Created especially for you

Date: _______________________________

Created especially for you

Date: ______________________________

Date: ___________________________________

Date: _______________________________

Created especially for you

Date: _______________________________

Created especially for you

Date: _______________________

Created especially for you

Date: _______________________

Created especially for you

Date: ___________________________

Date: _______________

Date: _______________________

____

____

____

____

____

____

____

____

____

____

____

____

____

____

____

____

____

Created especially for you

Date: _______________________________

Date: _______________________

Date: ______________________

Date: _______________________

Created especially for you

Date: _______________________________

____

Created especially for you

Date: _______________________

Date: ___________________________

Date: _______________________

Created especially for you

Date: ___________________________

Date: _______________________

Created especially for you

Date: ___________________________________

Created especially for you

Date: _______________________________

Created especially for you

Date: ______________________________

Date: _______________________

Created especially for you

Date: _______________

Created especially for you

Date: ____

Date: _______________________________

____

____

____

____

____

____

____

____

____

____

____

____

____

____

____

____

____

Created especially for you

Date: _______________________

Created especially for you

Date: ___________________________________

Created especially for you

Date: _______________________________

Date: _______________________________

Created especially for you

Date: ________________________________

Date: ___________________________

Date: ______________________

Created especially for you

Date: ____________________

Created especially for you

Date: _______________________

Date: _______________________

Date: _______________________________

Date: _______________________________

Created especially for you

Date: _______________________

Created especially for you

Date: _______________________________

Date: _______________

Date: _______________________

Created especially for you

Date: _______________________

Date: _______________

Created especially for you

Date: ___________________________

Date: _______________________________

____

____

____

____

____

____

____

____

____

____

____

____

____

____

____

____

____

____

Date: _______________________________

Created especially for you

Date: ______________________________

Created especially for you

Date: ___________________________

Created especially for you

Date: _______________________

Created especially for you

Date: _______________________________

Date: _______________________

Created especially for you

Date: _______________________

Date: _______________________

Date: _______________________

Created especially for you

Date: _______________________

Created especially for you

Date: _______________

Created especially for you

Date: ______________________________

Created especially for you

Date: _______________________

Date: ___________________________

Created especially for you

Date: _______________________

Date: _______________________________

____
____
____
____
____
____
____
____
____
____
____
____
____
____
____
____
____
____

Date: ______________________________

Created especially for you

Date: _______________________

Date: _______________________

Date: _______________

Created especially for you

Date: _______________________________

Created especially for you

Date: _______________________

Created especially for you

Date: _______________________________

____

____

____

____

____

____

____

____

____

____

____

____

____

____

____

____

____

____

Created especially for you

Date: _______________________________

Date: _______________________________

Created especially for you

Date: _______________________________

Date: _______________________

Date: ___________________________

Created especially for you

Date: _______________________________

____

Created especially for you

Date: _______________________

Date: ______________________________

Date: ___________________________

Created especially for you

Date: ___________________________

Created especially for you

Date: _______________________________

Created especially for you

Date: _______________________________

Created especially for you

Date: _______________________

Date: ___________________________

Created especially for you

Date: _______________________

Created especially for you

Date: _______________________

Created especially for you

Date: _______________________________

Created especially for you

Date: ______________________

Date: _______________________

Date: _______________________

Created especially for you

Date: _______________________

Created especially for you

Date: ___________________________

Date: _______________________

Created especially for you

Date: _______________________

Created especially for you

Date: ___________________

Date: ______________________________

Created especially for you

Date: _______________

Created especially for you

Date: ____________________

Created especially for you

Date: _______________________

Date: ____________________

Date: _______________________

Created especially for you

Date: _______________________________

Date: _______________________

Date: _______________________________

Date: _______________________________

Created especially for you

Date: _______________________

Created especially for you

Date: _______________________

Date: _______________________________

Date: _______________________

Date: _______________________________

____

____

____

____

____

____

____

____

____

____

____

____

____

____

____

____

____

Date: _______________________________

Created especially for you

Date: _______________________

Created especially for you

Date: _______________________________

Created especially for you

www.ingramcontent.com/pod-product-compliance
Lightning Source LLC
Chambersburg PA
CBHW071611150726
48000CB00004B/1672